THE SPACE BETWEEN THOUGHTS

THE SPACE BETWEEN THOUGHTS

A Reflective Journal

K.L. CARTER

*For every leader who forgot
they were already one.*

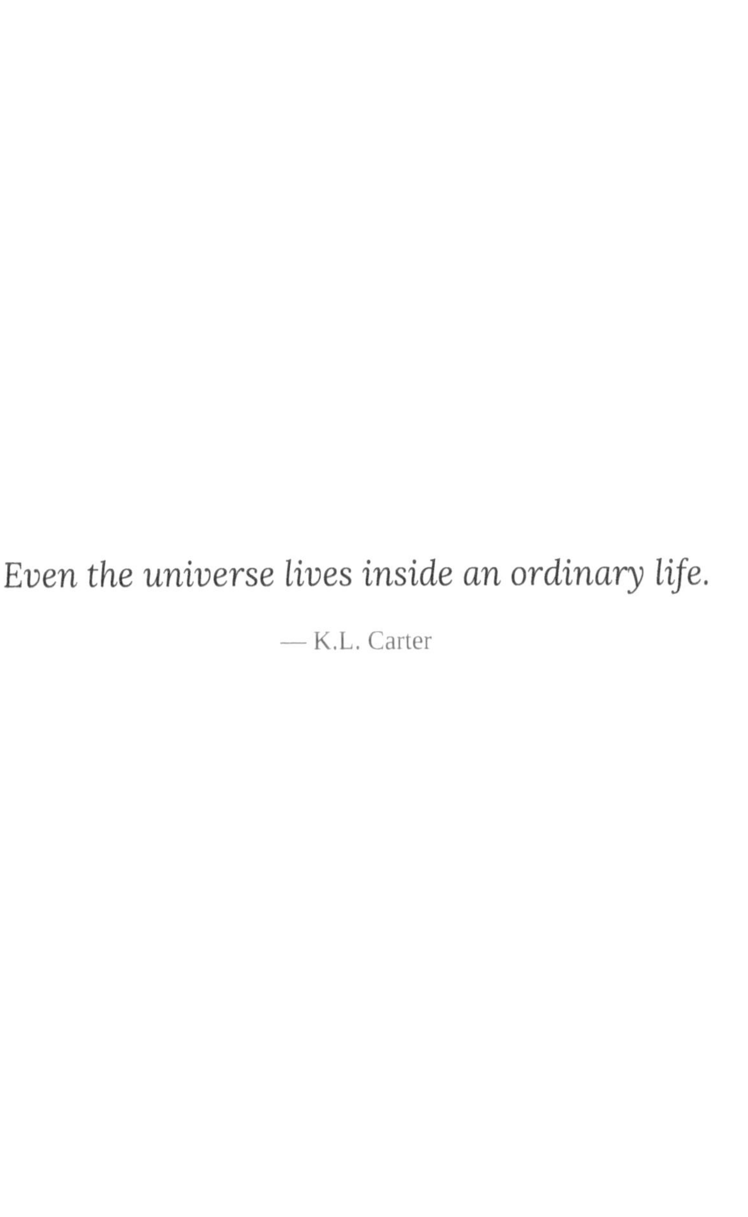

Even the universe lives inside an ordinary life.

— K.L. Carter

AUTHOR'S NOTE

I began sharing my writing publicly in 2024.

That may surprise people who have known me for years as someone who always had something to say. I have always loved to write. I have journaled, doodled in margins, kept gratitude lists, and filled pages privately for as long as I can remember. But putting that voice in front of a larger audience took longer.

Something shifted in 2024. I felt, with a clarity I could not ignore, that it was time to share more broadly. Not because the fear disappeared. It did not. There is always a quiet vulnerability in offering your thoughts to people you do not know, in not being certain how something will land, in wondering whether what moves you will move anyone else at all.

But I had spent years mentoring, facilitating workshops, holding conversations where I shared what I believed and watched something happen in the room. So I began writing it down more formally. First in essays and articles, then in shorter reflections, then in the affirmation posts that became a consistent part of how I showed up online.

What I did not fully anticipate was the return.

Sometimes it came quickly: a message, a comment, a share. Sometimes it came months later. A quiet note from someone saying that a particular thought had stayed with them, that it had arrived at exactly the right moment, that they had not just read it but acted on it. That they had made a change.

Those notes changed something in me. Because those posts began as moments of seeking clarity for myself. Something would happen, professionally or personally, and I would feel compelled to put language to it. The fact that those private moments of clarity could become something useful for someone else felt like the truest possible reason to keep going.

And so I kept going. And eventually I looked at everything I had written and thought: these deserve a different kind of home. Not just a feed to scroll past, but a place to pause. A place where you can read something, sit with it, and then write your own response to it. Because what is a thought worth if it does not move toward action?

That is the premise of this journal.

I have worked for over twenty years in an industry built entirely on the belief that the impossible is only impossible until it is not. That dreaming at the edge of what is known is not recklessness. It is the beginning of everything. These are reflections from the space between science and becoming.

This book is for anyone who leads. And you already do. Whether you work in space exploration or tend a garden, you lead. With influence. With intention. Often without a title that names it.

Leadership is not a title. It is a thread that runs through every page.

Sometimes all we need is a gentle reminder that we already carry what we need. Not a push from outside. A recognition from within.

— K.L. Carter

TABLE OF CONTENTS

Leadership is not a title. It is a thread that runs through every page.

PRESENCE

Where identity learns not to ask permission.

Presence does not require permission.

— K.L. Carter

There are moments when people wait for external confirmation before stepping fully into what they already carry. Yet presence is rarely granted by a room. It becomes visible when you stop negotiating your own place inside it.

REFLECTION

Where in my life have I been waiting for confirmation that I already belong?

From this point, I...

Your presence is your power.

— K.L. Carter

Power does not always announce itself through volume or force. Often it lives in how you enter, how you remain, and how you hold yourself in spaces that have not yet learned to expect you.

REFLECTION

What does my presence communicate without words?

From this point, I...

> # *I do not have to speak for the room to shift.*
>
> — *K.L. Carter*

---◆---

Influence is not always verbal. Sometimes the most significant force in a room is the one that moves quietly, occupying its space with full intention and no apology.

REFLECTION

Where have I underestimated the power of simply being present?

From this point, I...

Keep going. Be yourself no matter who is in the room, because your presence is the power.

— K.L. Carter

Not every room responds immediately to authenticity. Some require repetition before they understand what has entered. Still, authenticity remains lighter to carry than performance.

REFLECTION

Where do I feel most like myself, and where do I still edit too much?

From this point, I...

Impact requires a point of view, not permission.

— *K.L. Carter*

——— ◆ ———

A clear point of view often arrives before agreement. What matters is not whether everyone immediately understands it, but whether it is honest enough to remain standing when tested.

REFLECTION

What truth do I already know that I need to trust more fully?

From this point, I...

Style is not the opposite of intelligence. It is the companion to confidence.

— K.L. Carter

Expression and intellect are not competing forces. The fullest version of confidence often holds both simultaneously without apology and without explanation.

REFLECTION

Where do I still separate qualities in myself that actually belong together?

From this point, I...

STEM *is stylish. So am* I.

— *K.L. Carter*

The narrative that science and style exist in separate worlds was never true. The people who have moved both fields forward have always understood that presence and precision coexist.

REFLECTION

What part of my identity have I been told does not fit together, and what do I know to be true instead?

From this point, I...

Authenticity over perfection any day.

— *K.L. Carter*

Perfection is a moving target that belongs to no one. Authenticity is always available. The imperfect, honest version of you will outlast the polished, performed version every single time.

REFLECTION

Where am I waiting to be perfect before I allow myself to show up fully?

From this point, I...

1 Presence often arrives before confidence does.

2 Belonging is not always announced externally.

3 Authenticity carries less weight than performance.

4 Expression and intellect coexist fully.

II

GROWTH

What stretches eventually asks for room.

Growth often happens quietly.

— K.L. Carter

The most significant changes rarely arrive with announcement. They move through you quietly, rearranging things internally long before any external evidence appears. The absence of visible proof is not the absence of movement.

REFLECTION

What quiet change in me deserves acknowledgment right now?

From this point, I...

A healthy plant eventually tells you when the pot that once protected it can no longer hold what it is becoming.

— K.L. Carter

The pot that once protected the plant did its job well. That is worth honoring. And honoring it does not mean staying inside it when the roots have already pressed against every wall. Expansion is not ingratitude. It is the natural result of being tended well.

REFLECTION

Where in my life am I beginning to feel the pressure of necessary growth?

From this point, I...

Prune wisely. Bloom boldly.

— K.L. Carter

——— ♦ ———

What we remove is often as important as what we keep.
Pruning is not loss. It is intentional direction. What is released
creates room for what is meant to grow.

REFLECTION

What am I holding onto that may be limiting my bloom?

From this point, I...

There is a difference between refinement and erosion. A difference between feedback and quiet diminishment.

— K.L. Carter

There is language that sharpens you and language that slowly reduces you. Learning the difference is one of the most important forms of discernment available. Refinement leaves you more fully yourself. Erosion leaves you less.

REFLECTION

What kind of language helps me grow, and what kind slowly makes me smaller?

From this point, I...

From old rhythms to new purpose.

— *K.L. Carter*

Growth often requires releasing familiar patterns, not because they were wrong, but because they were designed for an earlier version of you. New purpose sometimes asks for new rhythms entirely.

REFLECTION

What old rhythm am I ready to release in service of new purpose?

From this point, I...

Not every season asks for bloom. Some ask for root.

— K.L. Carter

◆

Visible progress is not the only form of progress. Root seasons are quieter, less celebrated, and often essential. What grows deep eventually stands firm.

REFLECTION

What root work deserves more respect and patience in my life right now?

From this point, I...

It's your journey.

— K.L. Carter

Comparison interrupts progress. Other timelines are not your timeline. Other paths are not your path. The most honest work you can do is the work of following what is specifically true for you.

REFLECTION

Where have I measured my journey against someone else's, and what do I know when I stop comparing?

From this point, I...

Growth and belonging are not always the same thing.

— K.L. Carter

Outgrowing a space that once held you well is not a failure of that space or of you. Growth changes the fit before it changes the form. What once felt right eventually feels constraining, and that pressure is information worth listening to.

REFLECTION

Where have I confused outgrowing something with losing something?

From this point, I...

Sometimes the roots know before the mind does.

— K.L. Carter

The body and the deep self often understand what is happening long before the intellect catches up. Learning to trust that early knowing is one of the quieter forms of wisdom.

REFLECTION

Where is my deeper self already aware of something my mind has not yet accepted?

From this point, I...

1   Growth often becomes visible only after pressure appears.

2   Not every container remains right forever.

3   Pruning and blooming are part of the same process.

4   Invisible growth still matters.

III

LIGHT

What remains visible even in quietness.

Her journey was never linear, but always luminous.

— K.L. Carter

Linearity is often a standard imposed from outside. The actual path of meaningful work rarely moves in a straight line. It moves toward what is true, which is its own form of luminosity.

REFLECTION

What non-linear part of my journey has actually been leading somewhere important?

From this point, I...

Every star shines in its own way. So do you.

— K.L. Carter

Comparison often interrupts gratitude for what is already distinct. Difference is not deficiency. It is design. What you carry is not less because it does not look like what someone else carries.

REFLECTION

What quality in me deserves recognition without comparison?

From this point, I...

Stars don't dim their light. Why should you?

— *K.L. Carter*

——— ✦ ———

Brightness does not require apology. There is no version of humility that asks you to become less than what you are. Dimming yourself does not make the room brighter. It simply leaves your light unused.

REFLECTION

Where have I been dimming myself, and what would it look like to stop?

From this point, I...

Brilliant. Bold. Boundless.

— K.L. Carter

These are not aspirations. They are descriptions. Brilliance is something you inhabit. Boldness is movement despite fear. Boundlessness is what remains when limits are understood to be temporary.

REFLECTION

Which of these three do I most need to claim as my own today?

From this point, I...

Your crown doesn't need an introduction. It's always with you.

— K.L. Carter

You do not have to announce your worth before entering a room. The crown is not something you put on for certain occasions. It travels with you. It has always been there.

REFLECTION

Where have I been waiting for the right moment to walk in fully as myself?

From this point, I...

Not everything beautiful must be made dangerous in order to be respected.

– K.L. Carter

There is a persistent and incorrect assumption that softness must be hardened before it deserves acknowledgment. Elegance, warmth, and grace carry their own authority. They do not require conversion.

REFLECTION

Where have I felt pressure to make myself harder in order to be taken seriously?

From this point, I...

You belong in any space you are curious enough to explore.

– K.L. Carter

———— ◆ ————

Curiosity is its own credential. The willingness to explore, to ask, to remain in the discomfort of not yet knowing, that belongs everywhere. Belonging begins with the decision to show up.

REFLECTION

What space am I curious about that I have not yet allowed myself to fully enter?

From this point, I...

Light forms long before it is seen. Radiance rises from within. Emergence takes time.

— K.L. Carter

Brightness develops privately before it becomes visible to others. What is forming in you right now may have no outward evidence yet. That does not make it less real. Light does not wait for an audience before it begins to exist.

REFLECTION

What part of my life is developing quietly before it becomes visible to others?

From this point, I...

> *My presence is proof that the universe dreams in color.*
>
> — K.L. Carter

———— ♦ ————

Existence itself often carries meaning before accomplishment begins. You do not have to earn the right to take up space. Your presence is already evidence of possibility.

REFLECTION

What does my presence represent beyond what I produce or achieve?

From this point, I...

Your light makes space for others.

— K.L. Carter

True brightness does not diminish what surrounds it. It often gives others permission to stand more fully in themselves. When you shine without apology, you make it easier for others to do the same.

REFLECTION

How has my growth or visibility quietly encouraged someone else?

From this point, I...

1 Light often develops privately before recognition arrives.

2 Distinction does not require comparison.

3 Softness carries its own authority.

4 Curiosity is its own form of belonging.

IV

GRAVITY

What carries weight without explanation.

Gravity doesn't ask.

— K.L. Carter

Certain forces do not explain themselves before they act. They simply move according to what they are designed to do. Your depth, your pull, your quiet authority do not require justification.

REFLECTION

Where do I need to trust my own weight more fully?

From this point, I...

Twirl in the gravity of your own joy.

— K.L. Carter

Joy is often strongest when it is not performed, only inhabited. There is a particular kind of freedom that comes from moving inside your own delight without needing it to make sense to anyone else.

REFLECTION

What brings me joy without needing approval or explanation?

From this point, I...

Imagination is our first spacecraft.

— K.L. Carter

Before movement becomes visible, thought often travels first. Imagination is not separate from science or strategy. It is the earliest form of both. Where thought goes first, everything else eventually follows.

REFLECTION

What idea in me deserves greater permission and more deliberate exploration?

From this point, I...

Chart your course. Check your data. Honor the truth.

— K.L. Carter

Emotion and evidence do not oppose one another. Both matter when clarity is required. The scientist and the feeler are not two separate people. They are the same person, using different instruments toward the same truth.

REFLECTION

Where do my facts and my intuition currently agree, and where do they diverge?

From this point, I...

Defying gravity was not rebellion. It was her natural pull toward the infinite.

— K.L. Carter

What looks like defiance from the outside is often alignment from the inside. When you move toward what is unmistakably true for you, the people watching may call it unusual. What they are actually witnessing is someone moving without asking for directions.

REFLECTION

What feels natural in me even when others describe it as unusual or unexpected?

From this point, I...

She learned that even quiet things pulse with energy.

— K.L. Carter

———— ♦ ————

Stillness is rarely emptiness. Beneath quietness, much is already active. The things that move most powerfully in a life are not always the loudest ones.

REFLECTION

What quiet area of my life is more alive and active than I have fully acknowledged?

From this point, I...

Trust yourself and write your vision into reality.

— *K.L. Carter*

———— ♦ ————

Language often becomes the first architecture of what later appears. Writing a vision down is not wishful thinking. It is the beginning of its construction.

REFLECTION

What vision deserves to be written down with full clarity and commitment right now?

From this point, I...

Scale back or ramp up? Choose you.

— K.L. Carter

Every decision point is ultimately a choice about alignment. The question is not always whether to go bigger or smaller. The question is which direction is most true to who you are and where you are going.

REFLECTION

Where am I facing a choice right now, and what does choosing myself actually look like?

From this point, I...

Joy finds me, and I create it too. I am both the light and the spark.

— K.L. Carter

Joy is not only discovered. It is also made. Through attention, through choice, through the daily decision to notice what is already present and to build more of what matters.

REFLECTION

What habits or choices help me actively create light in ordinary days?

From this point, I...

Smile often, laugh a lot, and choose wisely.

— K.L. Carter

———— ◆ ————

These three things are not small. They are a complete philosophy. Lightness and discernment belong together. A life that holds both moves with both warmth and wisdom.

REFLECTION

Where in my life do I need more lightness, and where do I need more discernment?

From this point, I...

Know the difference. Noise ≠ Signal.

— K.L. Carter

Not everything that is loud is important. Not everything that is quiet is irrelevant. The ability to distinguish between noise and signal is one of the most valuable skills in both science and in life. Learn what actually matters and respond to that.

REFLECTION

Where in my life am I responding to noise when I should be focused on the signal?

From this point, I...

1 Some forces speak through consistency, not volume.

2 Joy belongs to embodiment, not performance.

3 Imagination travels before movement does.

4 Lightness and wisdom belong in the same life.

V

ORBIT

What remains aligned and what must move away.

Their bias is not your burden.

— *K.L. Carter*

——— ◆ ———

Other people's limitations of perception are not your responsibility to manage, correct, or carry. You are not required to make yourself smaller so that a narrow view can accommodate you.

REFLECTION

Where have I been absorbing someone else's bias as if it were information about my worth?

From this point, I...

Lead with humanity, but never absorb disrespect.

— K.L. Carter

Compassion and firmness are not opposites. The most effective leaders hold both simultaneously, leading with care while maintaining the clarity that disrespect will not be absorbed as the cost of kindness.

REFLECTION

Where do I need to practice leading with humanity while also holding a firmer line?

From this point, I...

Compassion and boundaries belong in the same conversation.

— K.L. Carter

The false separation between compassion and limits has caused many people to believe that care requires unlimited access. It does not. The clearest acts of compassion are often the most boundaried ones.

REFLECTION

Where do I currently need both compassion and a clear limit, and what would that look like in practice?

From this point, I...

Dismantle dysfunction without becoming part of it.

— K.L. Carter

Changing broken systems requires remaining distinct from them. The moment you adopt the tactics of what you are trying to dismantle, you have joined it. The most powerful change-makers stay whole while doing the work.

REFLECTION

Where am I at risk of becoming what I am trying to change?

From this point, I...

Empathy without action is sympathy's lazy cousin.

— K.L. Carter

——— ◆ ———

Feeling what others feel is only the beginning. Empathy that remains only in the emotional register, without moving toward action, is incomplete. The full expression of empathy is what you do with what you feel.

REFLECTION

Where do I feel something clearly but have not yet moved toward action?

From this point, I...

Protect your energy. Close the door with grace, and move forward in peace.

— K.L. Carter

Closure is not always loud. Often the strongest exits are quiet, made not in anger but in clarity, not in reaction but in alignment. Grace in departure is still grace.

REFLECTION

What or who requires a graceful, clear exit in my life right now?

From this point, I...

Not everyone will meet you with grace. Keep going. You are built to rise, not react.

— K.L. Carter

——— ◆ ———

Rising is a deliberate choice about where your energy goes. Every reaction you withhold is energy returned to your own momentum. You were built for forward motion, not for every invitation to stop.

REFLECTION

Where do I need to choose rising over reacting?

From this point, I...

When they try to fix you in place, remember: planets move, stars shine, and the universe expands.

— K.L. Carter

Movement is natural. Expansion is not betrayal. Anyone who needs you to remain small in order to feel comfortable is asking you to work against your own nature.

REFLECTION

Where am I resisting necessary motion out of concern for how it will appear to others?

From this point, I...

Those unsettled by your shine were never meant to exist in your orbit.

— K.L. Carter

Clarity changes orbits. When you grow into the fullness of who you are, the distances that form between you and certain people are not failures. They are physics. What cannot travel at your velocity simply falls away.

REFLECTION

What have I outgrown relationally, and what would it mean to honor that honestly?

From this point, I...

You can be a watcher or a doer.

— K.L. Carter

Both exist. Both have their moment. But if you have a vision that is unmistakably yours, the most honest question is whether you are moving toward it or observing others move toward theirs.

REFLECTION

Where am I watching instead of doing, and what would the first step of doing actually look like?

From this point, I...

Don't absorb chaos. Bring clarity.

— K.L. Carter

When disorder enters, the instinct is sometimes to match its energy. The stronger move is to remain clear while everything around you is not. Clarity does not require calm. It requires intention.

REFLECTION

Where am I absorbing chaos that I could be responding to with clarity instead?

From this point, I...

If you're going to stir the pot, at least use a spoon.

— K.L. Carter

There is a difference between precision and chaos. If something needs to be addressed, address it with intention and care. Disruption without direction is just noise. Disruption with purpose is leadership.

REFLECTION

Where do I need to address something directly, and what would doing it with precision look like?

From this point, I...

Elegance doesn't argue, it exits.

– K.L. Carter

—— ◆ ——

Some conversations are not worth entering. Some rooms are not worth staying in. The most powerful response is sometimes the quiet one. Elegance knows when to leave.

REFLECTION

Where do I need to stop arguing and simply exit with grace?

From this point, I...

Your joy exposed them. No *further* action *needed.*

— *K.L. Carter*

———— ◆ ————

Sometimes your happiness is the most clarifying force in the room. It reveals who is genuinely glad for you and who needs you smaller in order to feel comfortable. Joy does not require defense. It simply requires you to keep having it.

REFLECTION

Where has my joy revealed something important that I need to acknowledge?

From this point, I...

1   Other people's bias does not define your value.

2   Compassion and limits coexist fully.

3   Dismantling dysfunction requires remaining whole.

4   Grace in departure is still grace.

VI

SILENCE

Where thought finishes speaking.

Pause. Stars do not rush to be luminous. They simply are.

— K.L. Carter

◆

There is no urgency in what is already becoming. The pressure to perform brightness before it has fully formed does not produce more light. It produces performance without substance. Stars do not hurry. Neither must you.

REFLECTION

What in me is unfolding without needing to be forced or rushed?

From this point, I...

Joy does not have to be loud to be real.

— K.L. Carter

Quiet joy often lasts longer because it does not depend on witness. The deepest satisfactions rarely announce themselves. They settle in slowly, with the particular weight of things that are genuinely true.

REFLECTION

What quiet joy already exists in my life that I have not fully acknowledged?

From this point, I...

It's okay to hold space for yourself.

— K.L. Carter

———— ♦ ————

The same care you extend to others belongs to you. Holding space for yourself is not selfishness. It is maintenance. You cannot give from what has been depleted without eventually arriving at empty.

REFLECTION

What does holding space for myself look like this week, specifically and practically?

From this point, I...

You are not lost. You are simply traveling between galaxies.

— K.L. Carter

Periods without immediate clarity often feel larger than they are. Yet movement still exists even when direction is not yet named. Between one galaxy and the next, you are still in motion.

REFLECTION

What transition in my life deserves more patience and less judgment?

From this point, I...

The intangible you is fleeting, beautiful, and unforgettable.

— K.L. Carter

The parts of you that cannot be measured are often the parts people carry longest. Your warmth, your particular way of thinking, the quality of your attention — these leave marks that no metric captures.

REFLECTION

What quality in me cannot be fully explained but remains deeply true?

From this point, I...

Even the universe lives inside an ordinary life.

— K.L. Carter

Wonder does not require extraordinary circumstances. It lives in repetition, in the daily, in the unremarkable moments that hold more than they appear to. The extraordinary is already present in the ordinary.

REFLECTION

What ordinary part of my life holds unexpected beauty or meaning?

From this point, I...

She is a universe all on her own, boundless, brilliant, and unbeholden to anyone's orbit.

— K.L. Carter

Completeness is not something you build toward. It is something you recognize. You do not need external validation to constitute a whole. You already are one.

REFLECTION

Where have I been waiting for external confirmation of something I already know to be true about myself?

From this point, I...

There is something on the opposite side of the universe. Don't get lost in its vastness.

— K.L. Carter

The mind can travel so far into possibility, worry, or wonder that it loses the thread back to the present. The universe is infinite. You are also here, right now, in this specific moment. Both things are true.

REFLECTION

Where has my thinking taken me so far out that I have lost touch with what is right in front of me?

From this point, I...

Sometimes silence is the flex.

— K.L. Carter

Silence is not absence. It is often the most disciplined response available. Moving quietly, staying focused, letting results speak without announcement — that is not restraint. That is mastery.

REFLECTION

Where would silence serve me better than words right now?

From this point, I...

Zoom out, breathe in, and let the stars remind you of your strength.

— K.L. Carter

Perspective is a form of restoration. When everything feels immediate and overwhelming, the act of zooming out — remembering the scale of what you are part of — does not minimize the difficulty. It restores your sense of capacity within it.

REFLECTION

What do I turn to when I need to remember my own strength?

From this point, I...

The cup is refillable, not disposable.

— K.L. Carter

You are not meant to be emptied and replaced. Your energy, your peace, your presence — these are renewable. The question is not whether you have enough left to give. The question is whether you have been refilling yourself along the way.

REFLECTION

What refills me, and when did I last make time for it?

From this point, I...

1   Stillness is not the same as stagnation.

2   Quiet joy is still real joy.

3   Between clarity and clarity, you are still moving.

4   The extraordinary lives inside the ordinary.

VII

LAUNCH

The exploration never ends. Neither do you.

> *If someone else can't see your vision, that's okay. It simply isn't their dream. It's yours.*
>
> — K.L. Carter

A vision that belongs specifically to you was never meant to be voted on before it was built. The people who cannot see it are not seeing your dream — they are seeing the absence of their own. Keep building. Comprehension follows creation.

REFLECTION

What vision of mine am I waiting for others to validate before I fully commit to it?

From this point, I...

Create spaces where brilliance can breathe.

— K.L. Carter

When the environment that would welcome your brilliance does not yet exist, building it becomes part of the work. The spaces most worth having are often the ones that required someone to decide they deserved to exist in the first place.

REFLECTION

What kind of environment helps me think most clearly, and how can I create more of it?

From this point, I...

Her soul, a nebula of dreams, weaves starlight into reality.

— K.L. Carter

Dreams are not separate from the work. They are the first form of it. What begins as imagination, tended carefully and moved toward consistently, eventually becomes something others can touch.

REFLECTION

What dream of mine is ready to move from imagination into its first tangible form?

From this point, I...

She turned space into her stage, and every twirl wrote her story in the sky.

— K.L. Carter

The story you are writing is not only in the milestones. It is in every moment you showed up fully, every time you moved with intention, every choice you made to inhabit your life rather than observe it.

REFLECTION

What chapter of my story am I currently writing, and what do I want it to say?

From this point, I...

Even if someone else cannot see your vision, it does not make it any less possible.

— K.L. Carter

Possibility is not determined by consensus. The most significant things ever built were once invisible to everyone except the person who believed in them first. Your vision does not require a majority vote.

REFLECTION

What do I believe is possible that I have been afraid to say out loud?

From this point, I...

I don't exist to make stagnation look sensible.

— K.L. Carter

You were not designed for stillness that belongs to fear. Movement is your nature. Growth is your nature. Staying small to make others comfortable is a cost you should not keep paying.

REFLECTION

Where am I making stagnation look sensible when I know I am meant to move?

From this point, I...

Your dreams deserve a doer, not a doubter.

— *K.L. Carter*

——— ♦ ———

Doubt will always be present. The question is whether you give it the lead role. Your dreams are not asking for certainty. They are asking for someone willing to act in spite of uncertainty.

REFLECTION

Where am I letting doubt sit in the driver's seat of a dream that deserves action?

From this point, I...

Falling is a pause, rising is the victory.

— *K.L. Carter*

The fall is not the story. It is a moment in the story. Every person who has risen has also fallen. What separates them is not the absence of difficulty but the decision to get back up and what they carry with them when they do.

REFLECTION

What fall in my life am I ready to reframe as a pause rather than a permanent stop?

From this point, I...

Create your world; the universe is ready to meet you.

— *K.L. Carter*

———— ◆ ————

This is not a metaphor. It is a physics of intention. What you move toward, moves toward you. The work of creation is also the work of invitation. Begin, and watch what arrives.

REFLECTION

What is the one thing I am ready to begin, right now, from exactly where I am?

From this point, I...

1   Visions that belong to you do not require universal comprehension to be real.

2   The story you are writing lives in every choice you make.

3   Possibility is not determined by consensus.

4   The exploration never ends. Neither do you.

The exploration never ends. Neither do you.

— K.L. Carter

ABOUT THE AUTHOR

K.L. Carter is a physicist, aerospace engineer, and author whose career began at NASA Johnson Space Center supporting the Space Shuttle Program and the International Space Station, and has continued for over twenty years across various commercial and private space exploration endeavors.

She holds a BS in Physics from Southern University and A&M College and an MS in Biophysics from Cornell University.

For two decades she has worked in an industry built on the belief that the impossible is only temporary. That orientation shapes everything about how she sees human potential and everything about how she writes.

Katrina Carter-Journet began sharing her reflections publicly in 2024 under the name K.L. Carter, and what started as a personal practice of putting language to lived experience became something larger: a community of people who found in her words a quiet permission to keep going.

She is the author of the children's book Let's Chase the Moon and the affirmation books Earthium Rise Boy and Mystical Girl.

The Space Between Thoughts is her first adult journal.

She believes you are already a leader. She wrote this to remind you.